Original title:
The Necklace's Melody

Copyright © 2025 Creative Arts Management OÜ
All rights reserved.

Author: Ethan Prescott
ISBN HARDBACK: 978-1-80586-212-3
ISBN PAPERBACK: 978-1-80586-684-8

Secrets Beneath Shimmering Layers

Under layers of sparkle, stories swirl,
A squirrel in a tiara, what a whirl!
Dancing around, a feathered cap,
Who knew the jewels drew such a trap?

Fashioned for glamour, yet what a sight,
Mice wear pearls on an odd moonlight!
In the attic, the laughter took flight,
A dress of secrets, a sparkling fright!

Crescendo of Dazzling Echoes

Echoes of giggles, they bounce like light,
Whispers of diamonds that tickle the night.
A cat in a necklace, oh what a tease,
Wearing her jewels while stealing some cheese!

With every clang and clatter so bold,
Stories unfold that are worth their weight in gold.
Mischief makes music with every bright gleam,
In this symphony of humor, we dream!

Threads of Timeless Whimsy

Thread by thread, the tales unwind,
Of a snake in a bangle, how perfectly designed!
Spinning through frolics of laughter and cheer,
Who knew the gems could hum in your ear?

Worn as a crown by a grinning boy,
Each bead a secret, each stone a toy.
The fabric of folly, oh how it gleams,
We wear it well, stitched with dreams!

Glinting Crumbs of Heritage

Crumbs of history gleam and shine,
Chasing the puppy, he thinks it's divine!
What fun to discover, while digging for gold,
A spoon in the garden, a treasure to hold!

A parrot adorned in a glittery hat,
Preening for praises, just imagine that!
He squawks with glee, oh what a delight,
Inherit these giggles, let's dance through the night!

Threads of Gold and Memory

Once lost a jewel, oh dear me,
It rolled away as smooth as can be.
Chasing the shimmer with all of my might,
I tripped on a cat, what a comical sight!

The neighbor just laughed, they couldn't believe,
My dance with that feline, quite hard to conceive.
In search of my treasure, I found a new friend,
Together we snickered, the fun never ends!

The Tune of a Gilded Past

A bracelet of gold, it slipped from my grasp,
What a mishap, oh let out a gasp!
It bounced like a ball, what a funny spree,
I called it a dance; it adored the spree!

I chased it through stores, I ran with delight,
Past hats and plush toys, oh what a sight!
But the gem met its match in a bowl of hot stew,
Now it's more of a treasure, than it ever knew!

Reverie of Radiant Treasures

I wore my bling to the park one day,
Flashing my gems in a glamorous way.
But a pigeon swooped down, oh what a swoosh,
It mistook my crown for a cozy bush!

Chasing that bird, the crowd started to clap,
"Is it a show?" they cried, as I fell with a flap.
No riches in hand, just laughter and glee,
Sometimes the best fortune is just being free!

A Symphony of Silken Paths

A scarf made of silk, so shiny and rare,
Caught in the wind, it took flight in the air!
I ran after it, like a dog with a bone,
While onlookers chuckled, I looked like a clown!

As it danced past the trees, I leapt and I spun,
With each little flurry, the laughter was fun.
Finally caught it, oh what a delight,
Wrapped 'round my neck, oh so snug and tight!

Chants of Shining Belongings

In a shop window, they shimmer bright,
Bling and baubles, oh what a sight!
A price so high, oh what a thrill,
But my wallet shrieks, don't dare, be still!

With a twinkle here and a sparkle there,
A dance of objects, in the air they share!
Each shiny piece sings a boastful tune,
But my bank account hums a sad monsoon!

Enchanted Threads of Desire

A dress so bright, it calls my name,
The fabric whispers, plays a game!
I twirl and swirl in a fabric spree,
Checking the tag, it says: 'Not for me!'

With shoes that glimmer and sparkle anew,
I shuffle my way, in a magical view.
"Just one little pair," I plead with a grin,
But my budget laughs, "You know I can't win!"

Lull as Soft as Satin Dreams

Under covers of satin, I lay so snug,
But dreams of riches make my heart tug.
A gold-plated pillow, how divine it seems,
Yet I sleep on old fluff, not as grand as dreams!

Each night I prance in my fantasy gown,
Waltzing with jewels in a glittery crown.
But in the morning, it's back to the grind,
And my dreams of luxury are left behind!

Crescendo of Forgotten Glories

In the attic, treasures are hiding away,
Old boxes stacked high, in disarray.
A compass that spins, but won't find its way,
Alongside a hat from the 'fancy' ballet.

Once shining bright, now dust-covered scenes,
A feathered boa and Victorian means.
The glories of yesteryears, giggles abound,
As I pose and prance, what a laugh I've found!

Embrace of Dappled Light

In the garden, shadows play,
A squirrel steals my lunch, hooray!
Sunlight dangles like a tease,
While I chase it with the breeze.

Butterflies don't share my snacks,
They flutter off on graceful tracks.
Laughter blooms in every hue,
As I dance with a busy bee too.

A cat in shades of polka dots,
Takes a nap in tangled knots.
I trip on roots, the ground I'll greet,
But laughter makes it all feel sweet.

Leaves and giggles tangle tight,
As stars come out to join the night.
In this waltz of light and cheer,
Every fumble brings good cheer!

Tones of Fruition

Fruit trees sway with cheerful glee,
A lopsided apple grins at me.
Bouncing plums all roll away,
While I sneak in for a play.

Ripe bananas wear a hat,
Claiming this is where it's at.
Watermelons dance in pairs,
Spilling seeds and joyful stares.

Cherries giggle, bright and red,
As I try to balance my head.
In the orchard, joy's in bloom,
With fruit salad dreams in my room!

Each bite bursts with laughter's cheer,
Every fruit a friend so dear.
Under the sun, I swirl and twirl,
In this fruity, silly world!

Colors of Hope and Luster

Rainbows peek through rainy skies,
As puddles mirror our surprise.
With splashes bright, we stomp around,
In laughter's symphony, we're bound.

Crayons dance like fireflies,
On paper dreams, they sing and rise.
Sketching clouds and silly suns,
Each stroke a giggle, life's just fun.

A rainbow sprinkles silly tunes,
As giggles float like bright balloons.
Joy swirls in colors, bold and free,
Painting the world in harmony.

With each hue, a story grows,
Of laughter shared and happy woes.
In the palette of our days,
Hope glimmers bright in funny ways!

Weaving Stories of Forgotten Dreams

In the attic, old hats reside,
Each one whispers tales of pride.
A feather duster takes a spin,
With stories woven deep within.

Mice in jackets play charades,
As dust bunnies cheer in parades.
Clock hands tick in playful jest,
Hurry up, it's time for rest!

Grandpa's boots begin to dance,
Turning memories into a prance.
Spider webs weave a grand review,
Of forgotten dreams, tried and true.

Old trunks hide treasures made of light,
With silly socks to spark delight.
In every corner, laughter beams,
As I unpack forgotten dreams!

Hearts Entwined in Gold

In a shop with treasures bright,
A shiny piece caught her sight.
She grabbed it quick, no time to check,
But felt a tug, oh what the heck!

With every step, it slipped and slid,
She stumbled forth like a little kid.
Laughter rang, the town took note,
As jewelry danced, she lost her coat!

The storekeeper sighed, with a weary smile,
"Next time, dear, try walking a mile!"
She grinned and twirled, a brilliant show,
That golden charm, oh where did it go?

At day's end, with empty hands,
Still, her heart sang in merry bands.
For in the chase, so light and bold,
She found her joy, not diamonds or gold!

Cadence of Charm and Regret

She donned the piece with flair and grace,
A twinkle bright upon her face.
But every jingle, every clink,
Made folks glance, and pause to think.

A pigeon cooed as she walked by,
Its head cocked like it might cry.
Little did she know what it planned,
That shiny thing took flight, so grand!

"Hey! Come back!" she yelled in vain,
Chasing birds led to much disdain.
Laughter bubbled from every street,
As charm took flight, oh what a feat!

With each regret, she learned a tune,
Sometimes laughter bursts mid-afternoon.
For in her heart, she guessed it right,
The humor sparkles, pure delight!

Landscape of Shimmering Dreams

Walking through a shining fair,
She found a dream, with pizzazz to spare.
But in a game of hide and seek,
It vanished fast, her look was bleak.

Around the stalls, like a frisky fish,
It twinkled bright, a daring wish.
Friends were laughing, pointing loud,
She spun in circles, quite the crowd!

A jester juggled as she slipped,
One shiny orb was smartly gripped.
Both twinkled bright, oh what a pair,
Creating chaos, laughter in the air!

At sunset's glow, she pondered deep,
Such shiny things, too hard to keep.
Yet joy remained, in every gleam,
Life's laughter was her truest dream.

The Jangle of Dreams Unfolded

She stepped on stage with heart so bold,
A jangle bright, the crowd was sold.
But as she danced, the charm unwound,
A slip and slide became her sound!

The audience roared, their eyes agleam,
As jewels flew like a darting dream.
Laughter echoed, it filled the hall,
Her perfect plans went to free-for-all!

In the chaos, a friend would cheer,
"Who knew a dance could bring such cheer?"
With each new twist, her heart would sing,
In jangled dreams, she found her wing.

So laugh with me, as life unfolds,
In shiny moments, pure values hold.
For in the dance, and in the song,
We find our rhythm, where we belong!

Chaotic Beauty of Shining Sorrows

In a box quite plain and small,
Lives a treasure that could enthrall.
It sparkles bright, yet leads to woes,
Like a cat in boots, it strikes a pose.

A party planned, what could go wrong?
With jewels glinting, we dance along.
But hairpins fly, and drinks take flight,
Turns out the bling is quite a sight!

Yet laughter rings despite the fuss,
When friends all gather without a fuss.
Adventures born from glimmers lost,
In the chaos, we count the cost.

So wear your woes like a gown of glee,
Embrace the mess, dance wild and free.
For in the chaos we find our song,
A beauty hidden where we belong.

Beyond the Gleam

Glittering gems, oh so bright,
They promise dreams on a starry night.
But look too close, and what you'll find,
Is tangled stories left behind.

A yearning heart makes silly plans,
In a hurry, we can lose our fans.
The magic's here but not so fair,
As a dog wearing pearls throws its hair.

Beneath that shine, the truth unfolds,
Not every treasure is made of gold.
We laugh and shudder at that plight,
As mishaps dance in moonlight bright.

So lift a glass, and toast to fate,
For life's a show with twists ornate.
Dance with folly, lose all shame,
In a world where laughter is the game.

A Tune of Hidden Treasures

Sing a tune of joy and jest,
For shiny things might not be best.
They promise glimmer, spice, and zing,
But oh, the trouble they can bring!

A charm misplaced, a shoe untied,
While through the crowd, we have to glide.
A tangle here and a tangle there,
It's all good fun, a comedy affair!

With chaos reigning, hats askew,
We strut along, all shiny too.
A laugh escapes—let's own the scene,
A treasure hunt with a goofy sheen.

So gather round, and we'll agree,
In shiny blunders, we find glee.
For every sparkle hides a jest,
And in our laughter, we are blessed.

Threads of Memory

Little blunders, oh how they gleam,
Like a lost sock, they weave a dream.
In tangled tales, we find the glue,
Of laughter shared 'twixt me and you.

With every sparkle that catches light,
A memory dances, oh what a sight!
But beware the woes that sneak up fast,
Like hiccups at a dinner party blast.

An earring drops, a shirt unwinds,
While friend becomes foes—oh, never mind!
In bonds like these, true fun is told,
Where every stumble's a joy to behold.

So gather your friends, let the tales be spun,
In threads of laughter, we will run.
For life's a tapestry, bright and bold,
With every mishap, a story unfolds.

Portraits in Gemstone Hues

A ruby's grin upon the shelf,
Said, "I sparkle better than myself!"
Sapphire winked with a bright blue gaze,
"Join me in this dazzling craze!"

Emerald chuckled, a jolly jive,
"With our colors, we feel so alive!"
Topaz pranced in a sunlit beam,
"Together, we'll create quite the dream!"

In a jewelry box, they dance and play,
Whirling in a glimmering ballet.
Laughter echoes, a joyful spree,
In the kingdom of gems, so wild and free!

A Waltz of Luminous Threads

In a grand ballroom, the threads twirled wide,
Satin giggled, silk tried to hide.
Velvet spun with pomp and flair,
Draping its style without a care.

"We're the life of this fabric ball!"
Chimed cotton, dancing down the hall.
Taffeta teased with its crispy sound,
While lace floated lightly all around.

With a snicker, each fabric pranced,
In this frolic, who could resist the dance?
A waltz of threads, oh what a night,
Twinkling laughter and colors so bright!

Spheres of Ambition and Elegance

In a shop of baubles, the globes made their claim,
"I'm the best; just look at my fame!"
A diamond sphere flaunted, shining so proud,
While others watched, utterly cowed.

A quartz ball chuckled, "Hey, hold on tight!"
"I've got the charm, the shimmer, the light!"
Rubies rolled their eyes, expressing disdain,
"We're all just marbles in this playful game!"

Bouncing in glee, they jiggled about,
Creating a ruckus, a joyous shout.
In the realm of spheres, fun's guaranteed,
Every sparkling moment, fueled by need!

The Ballad of a Timeless Embrace

In a cozy nook, diamonds took a seat,
"Let's share a tale, oh isn't that neat?"
Emerald added, with a wink and a laugh,
"I once wore a crown; it was quite the gaffe!"

A pearl chimed in, "I've had my share,
Of misfit outfits in evening air.
Once I dressed flat in an old, drab hue,
Only to discover, I was sparkling too!"

With laughter echoing, they scrunched in close,
Each gem's little blunders, they loved the most.
In this embrace, where stories unfold,
A timeless tapestry of joy retold!

Trinket Tales of Longing

In a drawer, a treasure lies,
A bauble glints, it winks and sighs.
Oh what stories it could tell,
Of mishaps, laughter — all is well.

Once a plan to dazzle bright,
I wore it out, feeling just right.
But then it slipped, oh what a fall,
I chased it down — it laughed at all!

Through tangled hair, a chase so grand,
That shiny trinket held my hand.
We danced through puddles, splashed with glee,
My heart was light, but not my knee!

Now it sits, a rogue still speaking,
With giggles, our little secrets leaking.
A plastic charm, my fickle dream,
But oh, it shines when friends all beam!

Chiming Hearts and Hidden Truths

A bell that jingles with a chime,
Reminds me of my lost prime time.
Hidden in boxes, it tells my tale,
Of silly moments, never stale.

Friends once laughed at my grand plan,
To wear it out, my luck began.
It clinked and clanged, a rather loud fuss,
While I pretended, oh what a plus!

A night of dancing, heels so high,
That trinket flew, oh me, oh my!
I ran in circles, dodging my fate,
A glimpse of laughter, the price of great!

The secrets held, now long since spat,
That bell still rings, imagine that!
With each bright jingle, a chuckle's embrace,
A trinket's power, our funny grace!

The Dance of Light and Shadow

A glimmer found in funny light,
It danced around, just out of sight.
In shadows deep where mischief creeps,
It whispered secrets, laughter leaps.

Around my neck, one fateful night,
It caught the gaze, oh what a sight!
Laughter erupted, the crowd now swayed,
As I tripped over, a raucous parade!

To twirl in light was quite the thrill,
But shadows called, with hidden chill.
I stumbled forth, my status just low,
Can't cha-cha without a toe!

Yet through it all, the giggles fused,
With every tumble, the crowd enthused.
A sparkling charm still shines so bright,
In this dance of humor, we find our light!

Notes Carved in Elegance

A tiny note tucked in the seam,
Of elegance drawn from a dream.
It shimmies along with a wishful gaze,
To show off style in the silliest ways.

At a party, it aimed to impress,
With every flick and twirl, what a mess!
I twirled and waved, that gem caught air,
But down it slipped to a stranger's stare!

Oops, I thought, as they raised an eye,
My charm had fled — oh where oh why?
But laughter erupted, a blushing spree,
As I reclaimed my trinket free!

These notes of laughter, carved with jest,
In every sparkle, we find our best.
For elegance lives in a smile so bright,
When fun leads the way into the night!

Shimmering Echoes of Time

In a box of sparkles, lost and found,
A gem so grand, yet worth a sound.
Twirling in dreams on a string so light,
It danced in laughter, all through the night.

A mirror's glare, with a wink and a grin,
Each flash tells tales of where we've been.
With friends around, it's hard to resist,
That shiny trinket, too good to miss!

A giggle here, a chuckle there,
This trinket's charm is beyond compare.
But oh, the trouble of things we own,
That sparkle sings, a wildly grown tone.

So wear it bold, let the stories flow,
In shimmering echoes, let laughter grow.
With every glance, remember the jest,
For memories made are the true treasure chest.

A Chain of Heartbeats

A locket chimes with a beat so spry,
Each tick a laugh, oh me, oh my!
It swings from neck to a silly dance,
Poking fun at every chance.

In crowded rooms, it clinks and clanks,
While hidden glances exchange their pranks.
Plates are piled with seafood delights,
And that swinging charm steals all the bites!

With clumsy hugs and laughter grand,
That chain connects with a funny hand.
A tangle here, a twist over there,
In heartbeats shared, nothing can compare.

So wear it proud, and let it show,
A winding tale where giggles flow.
Each heartbeat's rhythm like a song,
In this chain of laughs, where we belong.

Harmony in Precious Moments

Under soft lights, a sparkle appears,
In whispers of joy and giggling cheers.
A bracelet with charms that jingle and sing,
Turning each moment into a zing!

With friends in tow, we dance and sway,
In this precious time, who needs to play?
For every giggle holds a bright glow,
This harmony's charm continues to flow.

Oh, the tales that each tiny trinket sows,
From breakups to laughter, as everyone knows.
With wrinkled smiles and tears in our eyes,
These moments shine brighter than any prize.

So let's celebrate the quirky delight,
In the rhythm of giggles, from day into night.
For in this treasure of humor and fun,
We find harmony—two hearts now spun.

The Cost of Jeweled Wishes

A ring with a glimmer, oh what a sight,
Promised more riches than a pirate's delight.
But with every wish, a chuckle rings clear,
Because bling can lead us to comedic fear!

From silly stories of slipping through time,
To tangled up chains that only don't rhyme.
What once was a dream, now wears silly shoes,
And every fortune comes with some funny blues.

Yet laughter prevails with each shiny spin,
As jewels remind us that joy comes from within.
So drop all the worries where they can't find,
These costliest treasures are whimsically blind.

For in this dance of sparkles and jest,
The funniest stories are truly the best.
So twirl with your jewels, laugh out loud,
In the wealth of your heart, forever be proud.

Silken Threads of Yearning

In a drawer, a treasure lay,
Whispers of love in disarray.
Sparkling dreams tied in a bow,
Yet, I lost it to a pizza dough.

With every toss, it danced away,
Caught in flour, gone astray.
Oh, the charm of this old thing,
Now it's just a doughnut ring!

I wore it out on my big date,
Hoping for love, feeling great.
But it fell right into the soup,
Dinner time turned into a loop!

Oh, silken threads that caused me woe,
You'd think they'd stick, but no, no, no!
Chasing dreams on a plate or two,
Both my heart and charm went askew!

A Memory Encrusted in Time

Once I found a gem so bright,
Adorned with memories of sheer delight.
But I lost it in my mom's stack,
Now it's buried, never to come back.

A shiny piece of grand design,
My friend found it in a wine.
Sipped too much, gave a twirl,
Now it's just bragging rights to hurl!

We laughed about its glittering past,
Wishing it was firmly clasped.
But glitter ends up in weird spots,
A dinner gag and lost thoughts!

When we toast with wine red,
I raise my glass, give my head.
For while memories twinkle and might,
They also hide in plain sight!

Timeless Resplendence

In a box, artsy and old,
Nestled gems and stories told.
Life's a party with bling galore,
But only if I can find the door!

I wore a bracelet with charms so grand,
Looked like a princess, took a stand.
Then while dancing, it slipped and bounced,
Now it's part of the dog's pounce!

Every sparkle comes with a tale,
Of rubber bands and runaway mail.
How could something shiny be so bold,
Yet vanish like a sneeze in the cold?

While I crave that timeless grace,
Life's a circus in this place.
With laughter echoing in delight,
Timeless magic takes to flight!

Beads of Enigmatic Allure

A strand of beads, so colorful and bright,
I wore them proudly, looking just right.
Then tripped on a rug, oh what a sight,
Now it's a jigsaw puzzle at night!

Beads rolled under the couch, oh no!
Like confetti at a party's glow.
Each little piece holds a whimsy tale,
Of goofy moments that never fail!

I searched high and low for that flare,
But they giggled away without a care.
All my charms became a race,
Time to gather 'em, what a chase!

Yet amidst the chaos and the cheer,
I can't help but laugh without any fear.
For every bead just adds to the fun,
A dazzling hunt for everyone!

Rhythms of a Hidden Jewel

In a drawer where secrets lie,
A shiny trinket caught my eye.
I wore it out to strut my stuff,
And felt quite fancy, oh so tough!

But as I danced, it took a leap,
My heart sank low, my face turned sheep.
It rolled away like a tiny star,
I chased it down, oh how bizarre!

The sidewalk cracked, it jumped in glee,
It surely thought it was so free.
I laughed and stumbled, what a sight,
A chase for glam in broad daylight!

Finally caught, my prize in hand,
I twirled around like I had planned.
But in the fray, my shoe was lost,
For fashion's fun, I paid the cost!

Serenade of Forgotten Glamour

In the attic, dust and dreams,
A gleaming gem with endless gleams.
I put it on for tea with friends,
But oh dear, where do the fun times end?

My hat was flat, my hair askew,
The jewel's sparkle brought me to rue.
It slipped and slid like a silly cat,
My guests all giggled, 'Look at that!'

It rolled off tables, around the room,
Like a cheeky clown, it brought such gloom.
But laughter echoed, bright and loud,
As I tripped on joy, a clumsy cloud!

By the time the sun dipped low,
I donned a smile, putting on a show.
No gems needed, just pure delight,
For laughter's charm was shining bright!

Lattice of Light and Shadow

A nighttime stroll, I found a spark,
In the garden, it lit the dark.
With a gleaming gem pinned on my dress,
I strutted proud, feeling no stress.

But then it winked, as if to tease,
And flew away on a gentle breeze.
It danced with fireflies, quite the scene,
While I just stood, a queen unsure, mean!

I ran and flailed, quite the ballet,
Twirling 'round, in a funny display.
Neighbors laughed from their porches wide,
For fashion's folly, they couldn't hide!

With a little dance, I gave a cheer,
The chase was silly, but I held dear.
In shadows low, my laughter glowed,
For joys like these are best bestowed!

Reverberations in Elegant Silence

In a quiet room, a shimmer calls,
A tiny gem with laughter sprawls.
I wore it proudly, feeling grand,
Until it hopped from my own hand!

It bounced on floors like a playful pup,
I leapt to catch, but fell right up!
Splits and slips became my fate,
While giggles bubbled, can't hesitate!

Under couches, behind the chair,
My grand pursuit turned into a dare.
Each time I reached, it danced away,
A cheeky jewel, come what may!

At last, I found it in the fridge,
Next to the pickles, what a bridge!
I laughed out loud, a fitting end,
For jewels and joy need not pretend!

Whispers of Glistening Dreams

In a drawer, a gem shines bright,
But it's just a plastic delight.
I thought it would bring me great fame,
Turns out, it's still the same old game.

I wore it out to a grand ball,
With friends who laughed at it all.
They said, 'It's quite a sight!'
But the truth? It's a total fright!

I twirled and danced, felt so grand,
Till the clasp broke—oh, wasn't it planned?
It rolled away, oh what a show,
Chased by a cat, oh no, oh no!

Now the memories sparkle and gleam,
Of a night that turned into a meme.
So here's to dreams that shine and fade,
And the laughter they've lovingly made.

Echoes of Adorned Secrets

There's a box with treasures untold,
Well, at least that's what I'm sold.
Each piece claims a magical tale,
But wearing them, I just turn pale!

A ring so big, it flexed my thumb,
I waved goodbye to that night's fun.
It flew off my hand in a whirl,
Landed right at an old man's curl!

A chain that sparkles, but it's a trap,
I stumbled, oh what a mishap!
"Fashionista," they called me with glee,
While I tripped over my own two feet!

But laughter echoes, loud and clear,
Such moments spark joy, with cheer.
So I'll wear my chaos like a crown,
In the kingdom of folly, never a frown!

The Luster of Lost Love

Once in love, I bought a charm,
Thought it would keep all harm.
But it slipped right off my neck,
And now, it's just an old wreck!

A necklace that promised the stars,
Ended up in my neighbor's car.
He said, 'What a find, I'm so blessed!'
I just laughed, 'You can keep the mess!'

Each sparkly piece held sweet dreams,
But now they're just colorful beams.
I've learned that love's not bling,
But the giggles that memories bring.

So here's to jewels we never keep,
And laughter that cuts oh so deep.
Lost charm, found joy, that's the score,
In life's vast game, I'll always want more!

Gemmed Reflections

I donned a brooch, a shining flair,
It winked at me with flair and dare.
But through the night, it popped and flew,
Sailing like a bird, oh how it grew!

'Twas caught by a dog, oh sweet pup,
He thought it was a toy to sup!
Chasing him down, I did a twirl,
Wishing my luck would unfurl.

The dance was a blur, laughter the tune,
With each hop, I felt less attune.
But in the chaos, joy did sprout,
As everyone cheered, "Spin it out!"

So here's to jesting gems galore,
Their mischief and giggles, we all adore.
For in this life, let us reflect,
It's the fun we find, we all suspect!

Serenade of Glittering Paths

In a shop of charms and bling,
A lady danced like a jester king.
With sparkles stuck in her hair,
She twirled and stumbled without a care.

A dog leapt up to steal a prize,
A shiny ring caught his keen eyes.
He dashed away with glee and pride,
While she just laughed and took it in stride.

Her friends arrived, each with a flair,
Trading tales of treasures rare.
Yet all that glittered made her pine,
For snacks and drinks, oh, how divine!

At nightfall's glimmer, all did cheer,
While the neighbors cringed, half in fear.
For laughter echoed, skies turned bright,
In paths of glitter, all felt right.

Nightingale's Adornment Song

A nightingale perched on a fence,
Adorned in jewels — quite immense!
With each sweet note, he caused a stir,
'Twas his shiny gear that made them purr.

The sparrows squawked in sheer delight,
"Where'd you get those gems so bright?"
"Oh, I found them near the stream!"
Said the bird, lost in his dream.

But as he strutted, clouds rolled in,
And raindrops washed away his bling.
With no more sparkle, he just croaked,
But his funny antics still evoked.

In the meadow, all did sing,
Of the bird who lost his shiny swing.
Yet deep inside, he knew for sure,
It's not the bling, but smiles we procure!

Legacy of Forgotten Lusters

In a dusty chest, old trinkets rest,
With tales of fame, they truly jest.
One locket winked, another sighed,
"What fun we had when we were prized!"

A clownish ring, lost at a fair,
Spun on his finger, without a care.
But laughter echoed from afar,
As someone mistook him for a star.

Those earrings once danced, now lie still,
Remarking, "Oh, if we had our will!"
In shadows, they chuckle — oh, what a sight!
Remembered fondly, as they took flight.

Yet the owner, caught up in the norm,
Brought out a jar to give them form.
With a laugh and a wink, they twinkled bright,
In memories' corners, still holding tight.

Tales Strung Along Twilight

As twilight fell, stories entwined,
A group of gems in a drawer confined.
Their whirs and whispers filled the air,
"Remember when we went square dancing with flair?"

A bracelet exclaimed, "The glittery ball!"
"When the folks laughed and tripped, what a fall!"
They giggled and jangled, sharing their days,
Painting the night in a funny haze.

Circus rings clinked, sharing their glee,
"Best dressed? We were — can't you see?"
But one rough stone spoke from the back,
"Sometimes being real means we don't lack!"

Under the stars, as the stories blend,
Twinkling and laughing, they'd never end.
In shiny camaraderie, they spin the night,
Tales strung along, all feels just right.

Murmurs of Filigree Reveries

In a shop of glimmering dreams,
The trinkets dance with golden beams,
A lady clutched her lovely find,
But lost it all; oh, how unkind!

With sparkles flashing, she did prance,
Yet held her purse, not a chance,
The gems slipped out, a bravado tale,
'Till she was left with just the mail.

Each friend chimed in with teasing jest,
'You only bought it for the fest!'
Her laugh rang out, a playful tune,
'Next time, darling, save the ruin!'

The echoes of her folly sing,
In tales of what those treasures bring,
With laughter bright, she reigns supreme,
For every shine is but a dream!

Threads of Love in Lost Luminescence

A ribbon knotted, oh so tight,
In pursuit of beauty, what a sight,
But as she twirled, it came undone,
Her dazzling look? A floppy fun!

With every turn, her dress would sway,
The jewels jumped out, a wild ballet,
Her friends all gasped, then burst with glee,
'You sparkle bright, but can't you see?'

Each laugh a thread, weaving delight,
While pearls rolled away into the night,
A tale of love, in chaos spun,
A charmer lost, but still such fun!

In shimmering hues and flip-flops too,
She danced half-hearted, but smiled through,
For every mishap led to cheer,
In charm and laughter, she held dear.

A Story Wrapped in Luster

Once wrapped in satin, neat and sly,
She wore her jewels and felt so spry,
But one by one, they found their way,
To tumble down and ruin her day!

"Oh dear!" she shrieked as sparkles flew,
Each shiny gem, a wild debut,
With giggles ringing, she did sway,
Fashion's blunders on full display!

Her friends just roared, "What a grand show!"
"Dig through the fluff, look where they go!"
With luster lost and laughter found,
They danced again on unset ground!

In every chuckle, a tale was born,
From glitzy blunders, none would mourn,
For wrapped in jest, they'd toast and cheer,
To stories told, with loved ones near!

Melodies of Adorned Moments

Adorned in jewels, she took a glide,
Her sparkles shining, she felt the pride,
But with a twist, and a tiny slip,
She lost her bling, a funny trip!

As gems rolled 'round the dancing floor,
She tried to catch them, but found more,
Each sparkle bounced like they had fun,
The night, a game; their work was done!

Her friends sang songs, with mirth they beamed,\n"Your dazzling night is more than dreamed!"
Through laughter loud and tales so bright,
She found her joy in the silliness of night!

In every glance, a wink of fate,
These moments cherished, never late,
For melodies played in jest and cheer,
Adorned in love, they'd hold so dear!

Songs of Precious Threads

In a drawer lies a treasure, oh so small,
Where fashion dreams and chaos enthrall.
Each string a story, a giggle or two,
But where's the glamour? Just beads askew.

She struts in flair, a swag that's rare,
Yet tripping on lace, oh, what a scare!
Her bling shines bright, a colorful jest,
Who knew that fashion could be such a test?

With friends all laughing at the flair she chose,
You'd think it's magic, from her head to toes.
But in that moment, hearts are ever light,
Faux pas or not, it's a funny sight!

As the laughter flows 'neath the thin chandelier,
She twirls and giggles, releasing a cheer.
For in this life of sparkle and sheen,
The best kind of charm is laughter, it seems!

Harmonies in Moonlit Charms

A necklace swings as she takes a glance,
But what's that noise? A clink, not a dance!
With every step, the shadows seem to conspire,
To trip her up, but they can't extinguish her fire!

Under the moon, her jewels take flight,
Reflecting the giggles that light up the night.
With mess and mishap, she wears a big grin,
For every fall just lets new fun begin.

Her friends join in, a chorus of laughs,
In the midst of mishaps, she takes all the chaffs.
Each charm tells a tale, with a wink and a sigh,
Who knew that mischief could reach for the sky?

As moonbeams twirl in this crazy affair,
It's memories they weave, beyond compare.
In this melody of chaos, they find their tune,
For laughter's the song that plays till the moon.

A Dance of Lustrous Echoes

In a twirl of silk, she dreams of the ball,
But today her necklace decides to hang tall.
With every whirl, it dangles and sways,
Creating a symphony of silly ballet.

Her partner steps back, a look of surprise,
As the decorum uncovers its lies.
He swerves and he dodges, oh what a scene,
Who knew a dance could be so obscene?

Yet laughter ignites, with each little clash,
As they spin and they stumble, quite the panache.
"Just call it art!" she says with a cheek,
"Next fashion trend: the clumsy unique!"

With echoes of giggles bouncing off walls,
They dance through the night, despite all the falls.
For in every misstep, the joy will be found,
In laughter and rhythm, fun's ever abound!

Veils of Glimmering Fate

With layers and layers of shiny delight,
She wonders which pieces to pick for tonight.
A mishmash of colors, a true fashion fright,
But hey, if it sparkles, it feels oh so right.

As she dons the jewels, a mirror reflects,
A face full of glee, with bling that perplexes.
"Am I chic or a clown?" she quips with a smile,
It's hard to decide, but it's all worth the while.

Yet as she struts out, a bead hits the floor,
A comical tumble, cue laughter galore!
With friends by her side, they cheer her blinged fate,
In this wild parade, misfortune is great!

So here's to the trails of shimmering glee,
And moments like these that set our hearts free.
For in this grand show, we laugh and we twirl,
In the joy of the mishaps, our laughter unfurls!

Strings of Abandoned Beauty

In a box of treasures, oh what a sight,
A forgotten charm, shining so bright.
It danced in dust, a forgotten tune,
Once adorned a neck, now sings to the moon.

A laugh escaped, as I gave it a shake,
It jingled and jangled, made me awake.
Where's the lady? Oh, where could she be?
Yearning for elegance, just like a bee!

With tales of glory, it starts to confess,
Of grand fancies lost, and a bit of a mess.
It chuckles along, with a twinkle so sly,
For beauty, my friend, is never too shy.

So here's to the jewels, the ones left behind,
With stories to tell, oh they're quite unrefined.
A string of bright memories, all twisted in cheer,
Abandoned yet aiming to bring forth a tear!

Heartstrings in Gleaming Shadows

In the corner it lurks, all huddled and shy,
With glittery glances, it starts to comply.
A heart in the crystal, it winks and it wobbles,
It's a jester of jewels, oh how it gobbles!

It spins like a top, under slippered feet,
As I trip over laughter, then quickly retreat.
The glow from its gleam, it tells of a jest,
Of parties and gaffes, oh it's simply the best!

With a twist of its chain, it starts to confide,
Of blunders and bling when wearers had pride.
It nudges my elbow, oh what a surprise,
The laughter it brings, it wipes teary eyes.

So raise a glass high, to the light that it holds,
For every misstep, a new story unfolds.
Heartstrings are tugged, not by love but by fun,
In shadows we dance, till the night comes undone!

Fables of Radiant Twilight

In twilight's embrace, a trinket awakes,
With giggles and sparkles, it jests and it quakes.
A fable of folly, all wrapped in a dream,
It tells tales of whimsy, like a lost sunny beam.

It sparkles with laughter, oh what a show,
A yarn spun in twinkles, a whimsical glow.
With each twist and turn, it captures our glee,
As we dance with delight, like leaves in a spree.

Its stories are silly, of times gone astray,
When one wore it boldly, then lost it one day.
It chuckles with glee, for the fun never stops,
In this twilight fantasy, where everyone hops!

So let's gather round, in this twilight's embrace,
With fables of laughter, we'll dance in this place.
For beauty not worn, can still shine and gleam,
In tales that we tell, like the sweetest of dreams!

A Tangle of Glistening Wishes

In a tangle of dreams, a wish starts to play,
With glistening giggles, in a whimsical sway.
A charmed little bauble, once lost in the throng,
Now hums a soft ditty, a jester's sweet song.

It winks from the shadows, with a grin so bright,
As it spins around stories, bringing pure light.
With wishes like fireflies, that dance in the air,
Each flicker a promise, a sparkle so rare.

The laughter it offers, a gleam in the dark,
Of moments so silly, like dogs chasing bark.
It twirls and shimmies, on memories made,
A treasure unguarded, that should never fade.

So here's to the wishes, all tangled and tied,
In the glee of our hearts, they forever abide.
For jewels need not shimmer, to dance with delight,
In a world full of laughter, they glow through the night!

www.ingramcontent.com/pod-product-compliance
Lightning Source LLC
Chambersburg PA
CBHW062113280426
43661CB00086B/605